Angels in Faded Jeans

W9-BGK-862

To her surprise, she discovered that her students were sensitive, creative, sometimes confused . . . and often hurting.

Angels in Faded Jeans

Käaren Witte

Jeremy Books

5624 Lincoln Drive, Minneapolis, Minnesota 55436

Photography by Vicki Hesterman

Jeremy Books

5624 Lincoln Drive, Minneapolis, MN 55436

Angels in Faded Jeans
Kaaren Witte

Copyright © 1979 Jeremy Books

Photography copyright © Vicki Hesterman

All rights reserved. No part of this book maybe reproduced in any form, except for the inclusion of brief quotations in a review, without permission in writing from the publisher.

Printed in the United States of America

Library of Congress Catalog Card Number: 79-84795

ISBN 0-89877-007-6

SECOND EDITION 1979

Foreword

Käären Witte is an unusual and delightful young woman. These true stories about her teaching experiences reflect an inner strength based on faith in her Lord, and an inspiring ability to see beauty and promise in other people—even the "different ones."

Her stories capture the exuberance and innocence of youth, as well as the pain, belligerence and sensitivity that often surface as adolescents face a fast-moving world.

Käären's "I believe in you, and in what you can become" attitude is refreshing . . . and infectious.

The Publishers

Acknowledgments

Thank you to Ruth Peterman, a great inspirational writing teacher.

Dedication

To Dad, who always believed in me and drove a million miles and stood on his feet for 25 years so I could become a teacher.

To Mom, who now waits for me with Jesus.

PHOTOGRAPHS INCLUDED IN THIS BOOK DO NOT DEPICT ANY OF THE ACTUAL SUBJECTS OF THE STORIES, BUT WERE CHOSEN TO ILLUSTRATE TEENAGERS IN GENERAL.

Contents

Junior High Is . . .

Jr. High is when you and your date have to get a ride with your older brother while he's delivering pizzas in a truck.

Jr. High is telling your substitute teacher that the mound of grass on the school lawn is "The Tomb of the Unknown Substitute."

Jr. High is believing all people over 25 use Polygrip and wear sensible shoes.

Jr. High is chewing gum and looking like a cement mixer.

Jr. High is thinking the only important quality in a boy is "cute."

Jr. High is when you think the guy who plays football, knows five chords on the guitar, and dates a cheerleader will be a sure success in life, and the kid who actually reads the textbooks, watches "Meet the Press," and writes letters to the editor is doomed to be a failure.

Jr. High is when a "Five Day Miracle Diet Plan" consists of two Snickers, 1 bag of nacho cheese chips, three Cokes and eight glasses of water.

Jr. High is when you think you can buy milk with your mom's credit card.

Jr. High is copying the poem "Trees" and thinking your teacher will believe you wrote it.

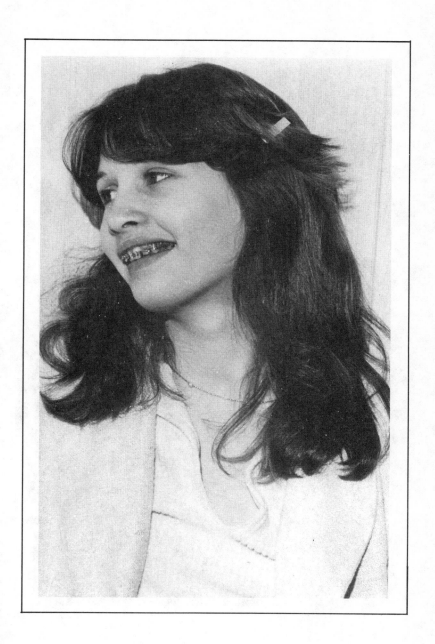

Suggestions from the Teenagers

At the beginning of each year, I ask my students to write down any concerns, fears, or suggestions. A few students once asked to work together and came up with this list of suggestions for me:

Please don't try to discipline us by humiliating us and cutting us down, especially in front of the other kids. (We will hate you for it. And we'll get back at you.)

Don't be a coward. You've got to believe you can handle us. (We'll test you, of course, and we hope you win.)

Be a nice teacher every day. Don't be friendly one day and a grouch the next. It makes us nervous and scared.

If we don't do the work, fail us. We want you to push us. Sure, we might kick and scream, but don't give in to us. (Be smart.)

Maybe you've heard bad things about some of us already. Could you erase those things? Think of us all as clones of Albert Einstein!

Please don't pooh-pooh our problems. (When some-body's dog dies, he might feel like dying, too. And when somebody we like says they don't like us, it is a BIG HURT to us.)

Please don't be afraid to laugh. A lot of teachers think we will take advantage of them and they'll have a rowdy class. But we won't.

Sometimes teachers do things wrong, too. Please have the guts to tell us you're sorry. (You will look big in our eyes.)

When you find out some of us aren't smart and can't read too good, maybe we could do other things good. (Sometimes teachers and parents make you want to kill yourself because you're not a good reader.)

Lord, Make Me the Teacher I Should Be

A teacher who laughs easily and loves the slow learners.

A teacher who has time to talk when she meets the kids at the Dairy Queen.

A teacher who doesn't take her weariness out on the kids.

A teacher who gives some hungry kid lunch money when he forgot his lunch ticket . . . (knowing it won't be paid back.)

A teacher who remembers a kid five years later . . . because she prayed for him.

A teacher who makes an unnoticed kid feel special.

A teacher who believes the kid others label a troublemaker will one day become a good husband and provider.

A teacher who spots one good thing about every kid . . . and lets them know it.

A teacher who takes a tall 13-year-old's crush on her much shorter boyfriend seriously.

A teacher that takes the time to write a personal note on top of every assignment . . . and not just a grade.

A teacher who treats every kid with the same respect and dignity as the principal or the president of the PTA.

A teacher who takes time after school to listen to the hurts and worries that come with being fourteen years old.

And most of all, make me a teacher who remembers what it was like to be young, and forgives kids for being teenagers.

LOVING THE WORLD
IS <u>NOT</u> THE PROBLEM...
it's loving the obnoxious,
foul-mouthed kid in
my sixth-hour class

Surrender for Victory

Did a song ever get stuck in your head?

As I dressed for school, I sang, "Victory, O victory is mine, if I hold my peace, the Lord will fight my battles. . . ."

By 10:05 a.m. this little chorus was stamped out. Elliot Kasindorft had just volunteered for his informative speech. I cringed as he made his way to the podium.

What will he pull now? Last time he said, "Here's my speech. Silence is golden!" Then he just stood there for a full fifteen seconds with a straight face until the class began to snicker. They realized Elliot was pulling a funny again . . . before I did. (*I* thought he would go on speaking after this attention-getting, dramatic quote.)

"Sit down, Elliot!" I had ordered.

He broke the silence. Throwing his head back, he laughed with manic glee and shuffled triumphantly back to his seat.

As Elliot continued advancing to the front, I thought to myself, "Would this scene happen again? Would a skinny thirteen-year-old make a fool of me again?"

If Elliot wasn't making defiant spoofs out of my assignments, he would be mouthing dirty words under his breath loud enough for some classmates to hear. Unfortunately, however, it wasn't loud enough for me to pin anything on him.

As he stood directly in front of the class, I braced myself for his anticipated flaunt of boldness. I remembered the time I announced a feature film by saying, "What other class entertains and amuses you like this speech and drama class?"

"Sex education!" Elliot blurted out.

The class laughed. I answered, "I don't want unsolicited comments—especially stupid ones."

Elliot smiled smugly, for he had delighted his audience both in content and in his spontaneous delivery. He was sure every kid would go home and tell of his brilliant comment at the supper table. Elliot seemed to savor the delicious thought of being immortalized in the minds of families across town.

I recalled the time I restated the policy of my class.

"You people know that whatever performances you do in this class must be done in good taste. There will, as you know, be no pantomimes on smoking, getting drunk or taking drugs. Since these are not a part of my life-style, they will not be a part of my classroom."

"What's wrong with smoking?" Elliot challenged from the last row. "It exists. We have a right to our own opinion!"

Some of his bold followers chimed in their agreement.

I wanted to slap his face and say, "You ignorant fool! What do you know? Your last diaper isn't dry yet!" But again I heard the words to that song: "If I hold my peace, the Lord will fight my battle. . . ."

"When you see a man coughing and choking from lung cancer, or a man with a hole in his throat, you'll see what I mean," I replied.

"Big deal!" Elliot responded as he rolled his eyes

and slumped over on his desk.

But now my attention went back to Elliot as he stood in front of the class again. They waited expectantly, and with a straight face and a pause, Elliot began.

"My topic title today is, 'How to stamp out sex in the locker room and save energy for sports.' " Two of his buddies cheered and whistled and a few girls looked embarrassed.

"Sit down!" I demanded.

Since I did not want to glorify the incident further by discussing it, I asked for the next volunteer.

As the class ended I stormed to the principal to demand that Elliot be taken out of my class. After all, I had my rights! I didn't have to put up with this animal! But as I reached the principal's office, those words raced across my mind again: "If I hold my peace...."

"O.K., O.K.," I reluctantly decided. "I'll hold my peace, but I am going to call Elliot's parents and tell them what a miserable, rotten kid they have!

"No doubt they will be defensive and insist that I am boring their creative prodigy!

"He may verbally abuse you and kick you around," I would tell them. "But he won't do it to me!" As I dialed Elliot's phone number and waited for one of his parents to answer, again the words of the song convicted me.

"O.K., Lord! Forgive this vengeance of mine! Fight my battle," I prayed as the phone rang a half dozen times. On the telephone note pad I scribbled, "Dear God: I resign."

"Hello, Mrs. Kasindorft. This is Käären Witte. I'm Elliot's teacher. I'm sorry to have to make this call, but he resents my authority." Then I began to list his offenses, but calmly.

"I'm so sorry you had this trouble," came her understanding voice. "You have such a kind voice and a sweet attitude. You don't deserve this. His father and I will speak to him. I'm so glad you called. Thank you so much for telling us."

The next day Elliot stood at my desk. Without looking at me he mumbled, "Miss Witte, I am sorry. I've been a rat. You didn't deserve it. I'm going to do better."

"Elliot, you are ten feet tall in my eyes today. It takes a *real* man to admit he was wrong and I admire you," I said.

He half-smiled in spite of himself as he went to his desk.

Just like the song said: "If I hold my peace, the Lord will fight my battles. . . . "

Left Out

"Hey! Skinner! Skinner! Your ears stick out! You got zits city, too!" one student said, taunting Jerry while giving him the cutting nickname of "Skinner."

"Skinner," another chimed in, "one of the cheerleaders loves you passionately!"

Jerry was a below average student in a class of whiz kids and at the beginning of the year this skinny slow learner was the object of cruel jokes. Kids always spot the least little thing out of the norm to pick on, and now they found Jerry to be an easy defenseless target.

Most pathetic of all, Jerry didn't even realize they were ridiculing him. He thought they were his friends.

One day in December Jerry was absent and I prayed as I prepared to talk with the class.

"Lord, God, help me to show your very love for Jerry to these kids. I see the persecution mounting. Jerry is bound to feel it soon. Do something through me; I can't bear to see this lamb mocked and devastated!"

The bell rang. I whispered, "Jesus, guide my words!" and taking a deep breath I began:

"You people have been cruel and cutting to Jerry. Maybe he was not blessed with as many brain cells as the rest of you, but you are showing your brains by picking on some little kid who is less fortunate than you.

You're only trying to make yourselves look big through these thoughtless, immature, cheap shots."

Every head was bowed, not one eye met mine.

"You will destroy a human being if this continues. Now how would that make you feel?" I continued as my voice cracked with emotion and quivered. "I know that you will be real 'men' and real 'women' and change all this. What could you all do special to bring a feeling of love and acceptance to Jerry? You decide among yourselves."

One week later at the Christmas party, I watched Jerry grow wildly excited with every name that was called out to receive the dollar exchange gift from under the tree. Jerry's cheeks got red and little beads of perspiration formed on his upper lip. His roaring nasal laughter grew with every name that was called. He knew his was coming!

The last gift was called out and the student playing Santa went to the hall. Jerry's face fell. The laughing noises stopped. He began to realize there was nothing for him.

He slowly got down from the chair he had been standing on. He looked in confusion once again at the tree before his chin started to quiver and his chest began to heave in sobs. He put his head down at his desk and continued to weep. I couldn't understand what had happened.

Before I pushed open the door to go to the hall, I saw that most of the class did not even notice Jerry. They were in small clusters examining each other's gifts.

"That's it, you guys! Get that box in there! He's crying!" I screeched to the boys in the hall who were trying to wrap Jerry's present.

(Did you *ever* see three thirteen-year-old boys try-ing to wrap a big box? Each was screaming out orders to the others. Then they'd lose the tape on the dis-penser. None had fingernails to get the tape off, either. While one would paper one end, the other would stretch the paper too far and pull it off. After each of the three boys attempted to make a bow, I grabbed the ribbon and twisted a red knot that vaguely resembled a bow.)

They squeezed the box through the door and pushed it in front of Jerry. A hush of expectancy came over the other kids.

But Jerry didn't stop crying. He didn't even look up.

"Tell him it's for him," I said to one of the boys.

He still didn't look up.

"Jerry," I whispered putting my arm around him, "the kids got the best present just for you!"

He then stared at the box. "Was he just going to yell 'Forget it!' " I wondered.

Slowly he reached for the box. Then he began to slash the green foil paper and tear the ribbon. His flushed cheeks and nasal laughter surfaced again.

Inside the box he found a Louisville Slugger bat, a white softball and a good baseball mit that smelled of new leather.

The class applauded and cheered.

My eyes were swimming. It was a touching scene in the classroom, but more than that I saw something else.

"Oh, Lord Jesus," I said silently, "this is just like You! I kick and cry so my eyes are swollen telling You how You have forgotten about me, but remembered everyone else. Then in Your

timing You bring something great...just for me!"

"Thank you, Father God," I said softly, "for showing me Jesus in my blackboard jungle one more time."

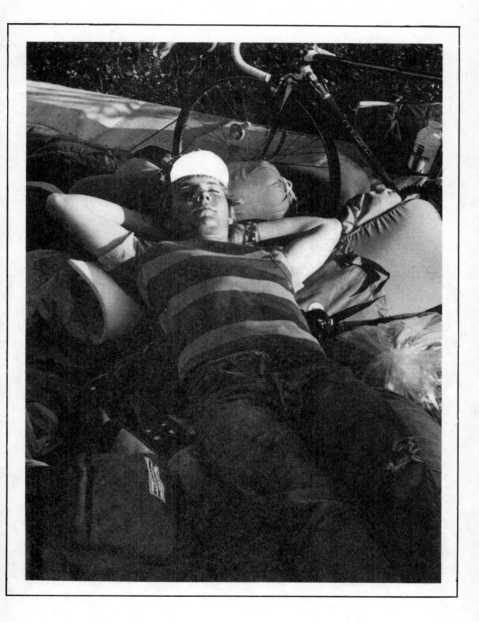

Dusty

"Hello-o-o, Miss Witte," Dusty would coo as he entered class each day.

"Hello, Dusty." I would answer, tripping into a more professional voice.

Dusty was one of those rare kids who was 5' 9" already at fourteen. He was the basketball star, and his thick blonde hair flapped as he dribbled down the basketball court. His glistening sweat complemented his Malibu-like tan.

"How can one kid have so much poise, confidence, warmth, brains and good looks?" I often wondered.

When kids were using rough language, Dusty would bonk them over the head with his books. "Hey! Don't talk like that, you idiots!" he'd say, motioning that there were girls present.

When the class would get too noisy he would stand up and quiet the kids down. He was a leader, and a well-liked young man.

After school, he would come into the room, push the papers off the corner of my desk and prop himself up, like a big dog—large and leisurely.

He said he loved the creative assignments I gave. And he would talk about the clothes I wore as well as which ways he liked me to fix my hair.

"What's the perfume you wear all the time? It's neat. I want to give it to my mom for Christmas," he once said.

I admired his manly instincts. At fourteen, he was protective and considerate of women.

"Here, let me help carry those books to the car!" he'd yell, running across the school yard. "Give me your key. I'll open the door. Say! It looks like you need air in those tires. Don't forget, because that's danger-ous."

Occasionally, I would find notes in my desk drawer or under the windshield wiper: "Have a nice day!"

Maybe I was wrong, but I suspected they were from Dusty.

Often, on his papers, I praised him and thanked him for his friendship.

In the spring of the year, I was signing Bob's year-book. Suddenly my eyes shifted to the next page where Dusty had written to Bob. I spotted my name and be-gan reading.

I was choking with emotion as I forced the tears to the back of my throat.

I slammed the book closed without finishing my message to Bob.

The words of some other teachers blasted through my mind: "Don't get involved with the kids" and "Kids will stab you in the back every time" or "Keep an arm's distance; you can't trust kids."

Dusty had written: "We sure fooled ol' Witte. She was a chump for a few smiles and warm fuzzies! I hope we have more like her in high school. These are the easiest grades we've ever got!!"

I knew I had two choices. I could believe the teachers were right and Dusty had stabbed me in the back. Or I could believe that he really was a sincere kid and this was just a thoughtless writing when he needed to look tough and big.

I decided to choose the second.

I opened the yearbook and drew a circle around Dusty's words. From the circle I drew an arrow to the bottom of the page and wrote: "Dear Dusty, I *still* give you my love and friendship. No matter what. It's a beautiful exchange. Love, Miss Witte."

"Jesus," I prayed closing the yearbook, "this is just like You. You risk Your love and friendship every second of every day for us. And when we come to You, You pour Your life into ours and give us all that You have. And what do we say when we come to You!! 'Lord! I give You . . . my jealousies, my envy, my past, my failures, and my hypocrisy.' And You always say: 'It's a beautiful exchange.'"

You are a plan,
waiting to materialize
You are a dream,
waiting to unfold
I believe in you because
your Creator, the God
of the universe,
made you special.'

Kay Isn't Cute

Kay, a gangling fourteen-year-old in my "blackboard jungle," has short, straight black hair and a flat, pushed-in nose. Kay doesn't have bouncing curls and her mother never puts bows or barrettes in her hair.

I've watched Kay sit through the year while other students worked enthusiastically on drama class projects. Sometimes Kay would just draw straight lines across a piece of paper and hum monotone sounds.

Kay often put her arm through mine while I stood in the hall, or she would put her arm around me and put her head on my shoulder. Her I.Q. is below average, and I often thought, "She is too dull to know that it is *not* cool to need or show affection for anyone... especially a teacher!"

Frankly, Kay bugged me! She was not smart and worse yet, she was not cute. Her hair smelled bad and she always stood too close when she talked to me, which was often. She usually had a dripping nose and a cold, and would cough in my face.

Kay annoyed me with such trivia as, "Mrs. Witte (she could never remember that I was single), we're going to make popcorn tonight." Or, "I saw you driving to school today."

Frequently, I had to be blunt with Kay. I had to push her away if she clung to me, saying, "Kay, I don't want the other children to think that I'm favoring you."

With a broken-hearted look of rejection, she would leave.

"Why does Kay annoy me?" I asked myself, "and why do I reject her? Of course my rejection is in the guise of being fair to the other students. But is that actually the real reason?"

It is *so* easy to love Eric! At fourteen, he's tall, tanned and attractive. Eric stops by the door before leaving class and waits until I look at him. Looking straight into my eyes, he smiles and softly says, "Goodbye, Miss Witte, and have a good day now." He then flashes a pearly set of teeth and a 500 watt smile!

When I talk to the class, Eric listens intently. He hangs on every word. Kay might be scribbling, and other students may be writing secret notes or pulling up their socks or pushing their hair back.

Not Eric. He makes me think I'm the Joan Rivers of the teaching set. He catches the funny little jokes that I enjoy making. Nobody but Eric seems to get them. He laughs and winks and flicks his fluffy hair out of his face. Because he has always felt accepted, admired and loved, he has the confidence to respond, so it is easy to praise Eric. But after all, he has been blessed from birth with good looks. Kay has not.

"All God's children are created worthy!" the Lord gently reminds me.

Kay deserves my respect, too. When she comes to my desk, she deserves that I stop writing, give her my full attention, and treat her as if she were the most important, adorable person in the world. Nothing less will do, according to God's standards. Doesn't He say, "If you've done it to the *least* of these, you've done it to me"?

"Jesus," I pray, "Kay must feel emptiness and pain. Why do I value the pretty child more than the unattractive one? How must Kay feel, knowing she is not cute? She must see icy, impersonal, steely eyes of rejection looking at her each day. Kay is not so dull she would miss them! She sees that the cheerleaders are those girls with clear complexions and perfectly shaped adolescent bodies. And the Spring Fling Princess is a slim, shiny-haired popular classmate. What does Kay use for manipulating and bargaining power?"

The other day, a teacher I know was talking about a child who had bargaining power because of her physical beauty. He said, "This little Peggy came up to me with those big, Bambi eyes and said, 'Mr. Olson, I had to practice for my dance line so I didn't get to study for my test. Do I have to take it?' She smiled, swished her long blonde hair and touched my arm affectionately. I melted."

At fourteen, Peggy already knew her power. Eric probably does, too. What does Kay use?

"Lord Jesus, help me not to punish ugliness and reward cuteness! Don't let Kay be a drop-out or a run-away or find acceptance in a gang that uses pot and pills in place of love," I prayed.

A verse from Isaiah often comes to mind as I teach:

"All thy children shall be taught of the Lord and great shall be the peace of thy children."

I have to be the arms of Jesus in my blackboard

jungle. He has no others. *His* arms would be out-stretched. *His* shoulder would be waiting for a needy little head.

Jesus sees Kay as beautiful as Eric! (Maybe more so ...)

Joy in My Mourning

"Miss Witte . . . I won't be in school today," Susan choked with emotion. "My mom died."

"Oh Susan," I whispered holding her shoulders. "I'm so sorry. I know how you feel."

I hugged her. And I cried. We weren't student and teacher. We were just two human beings that shared the deep cuts of sorrow.

"I feel so alone. I hurt so much. I don't want to live anymore," she sobbed.

Looking in her eyes, I said, "I know your mom is with Jesus. I prayed for her while she was sick and I knew she believed in Jesus like you do."

She nodded and pressed the wadded Kleenex to her eyes.

"Sit down for a while," I said, moving two desks close together. I took a box of Kleenex out of my desk drawer and put it between us.

"Susan," I whispered, "I stood alone at my mom's grave this fall the day after the burial feeling sliced, raw, and abandoned, too. I shouted and questioned God: 'Could I ever be a whole person again? Could Dad?' "

"Then God's Spirit came to me and said, 'She will be loved and cared for forever.' I began to softly repeat the name of Jesus over and over. The inner shock eased away. I don't know how it happened, Susan, but my empty heart was filled."

Susan stopped crying and interrupted me as she remembered a time when she and her mother got the giggles ... during her cousin's classical piano recital!

I was glad for her memories as I continued to share more.

I told her my mother's funeral had been in October on the kind of day she would have liked to go walking just to hear the crunch of leaves and feel the last brush of warm before winter.

" 'Some things are more beautiful dying, like leaves,' Mom once said. And I never forgot that," I shared.

"Susan," I continued, "Mom's death didn't make the six o'clock network news; only some obscure, small town newspaper obituary. But she did make one man feel like a king. She made us kids see Dad as a hero. She wasn't Mrs. America or in *Who's Who*, nor was she an award winner of any kind. She was just my mother whose life and death brought me closer to Jesus. So what greater thing could be said about anybody?"

"But I can only think of my mother dead and buried under dirt," she interrupted, weeping uncontrollably.

"Susan ... ," I pressed, putting my hand on her arm, "one day in the wind I whispered excitedly, 'Mom! What are you experiencing?!' Susan! we can not even imagine what heaven must be like when a child—like your mother and my mother—ransomed by Jesus Christ, comes home! These were people for whom Jesus was hanged on a cross—naked and dying. They are God's own children!"

"But I'm having trouble believing I will ever see her again," she choked.

"One day, Susan, our whole universe will be filled with rejoicing, adoration and singing—echoing from planet to planet. This is the day that the last enemy, death, will be defeated! And we will be reunited with our mothers!"

"Susan," I said now taking her hand, "I'll pray before the bell rings: Jesus, I give You thanks as we sit here for every tear, every hurt. These are the things that are helping Susan and me grow. Lord Jesus, You just use death to take us from one realm to another. Tell our mothers we miss them. We'll see them soon. We rejoice right now, because two of us are with You."

Then Susan whispered a prayer with just one word: "Jesus."

Just before she left, I opened my wallet and gave her a folded letter.

"This is a copy of the letter my mom gave me while she was dying. I know these were your mom's thoughts and words, too, because she knew Jesus."

After a quick hug good-bye, she left, stuffing the folded wad in her history book.

The letter said:

Dear Käaren,

God is calling me home and God is asking you to release me. Please don't cry anymore. When you cry, you will spread your sorrow to others. When you laugh and sing, others will be lifted.

Saying good-bye is our most painful assignment, but you know when I am no longer in this body, I will be with the Lord Jesus Christ.

We'll be separated for a short time. You'll see. Then we'll laugh and sing together again.

I will be there on your wedding day and I will be there at the birth of your own babies. Never doubt that.

I will soar with the same pride I've always felt as I've watched you become a young woman.

Continue loving and giving to your world. Love those I love and serve those who love me. Then you will always honor me.

Remember Jesus and I are closer than a prayer.

My love . . . forever, Mom

I'm Low on Love, Lord

I want to slap Gary up and down and shake that cocky snickering out of him.

His appearance says, "I hate this rotten school."

Wearing that unironed shirt and torn jeans, he flicks his shoulder length hair back.

He's defiant, smirking and mocking.

As You see, Lord God, I need Your supernatural love for this kid.

(What would my audiences say if they saw a "lovely, loving" speaker like me writhing in anger right now?)

I know that there's no hate, mine or Gary's, that cannot be dissolved by Your love.

Thank you that I can stand in front of You naked,

Knowing you will still love me—
Even when I am low on love for a kid like Gary.

I Want My World to Know! (Sometimes)

Humming the victorious song "To God Be the Glory," I breezed into the faculty washroom.

As I ran the comb through my hair, another teacher came in.

"Oh! I heard singing! I should have known it was you! You're the only junior high teacher I know who sings!" Lettie said, smiling at me in the mirror.

I held the door as I was going out. My mind raced for a response. "This was the moment. The opportunity. My chance." I thought. "Two seconds have passed. If I were sure why I was singing I didn't have to take so long to answer. I'll bet she's thinking that. I've got to tell her that Jesus Christ makes me sing! He has given me a new life!"

"No!" I panicked, "I can't say it like that. Lettie is the faculty swinger. I'm sure she thinks anything religious is hopelessly ignorant and naive."

"Say something!" I kicked myself.

"Ah . . . Lettie," I gulped, "I sing because . . . ah . . . I have hope! I mean a great hope!"

She continued to comb her hair without missing a stroke.

"She didn't hear you! Say it again, Dummy!" I yelled at myself before going out the door.

"Ah . . . Lettie, I've got hope!" I said louder this time and with a wink.

Lettie merely nodded her head and gave me an indulging smile. She seemed to be saying non-verbally, "I heard you the first time. So big deal . . . you've got some hope."

"Even the wink didn't give her slightest hint that the 'Hope' was Jesus Christ," I regretted, going down the hall.

"Jesus, I blew it for You. Why didn't I say Your name?? I want to have the same boldness to say 'Jesus Christ is my hope and He makes me sing—even here in school,' as I do when I speak to churches, youth groups, and banquets. I want another chance. For Lettie."

Hair Today, Gone Tomorrow

I didn't mind that one student had hair flowing below the shoulders. But when I found out the student's name was William, I flinched.

One day William came to school with cropped hair—his ears barely covered.

A growing circle of gaping kids shouted and fired questions at him. (They looked like reporters who had discovered a Watergate scoop.)

"Man! How did you do it??" one long hair demanded.

"I sat in the barber's chair after having my last meal and asked for a blindfold," he said, biting his lip remembering the horror.

"Oh! William, you shouldn't have . . . " wailed one girl.

William shuffled his feet and bowed his head in anguish. I went to his rescue.

"Think of it this way, gang. Now William can enjoy new advantageous things in life. Like seeing. And furthermore, there's the advantage of not eating hair!" I laughed.

(I laughed alone.)

"You mean all the time I complained about hair in my food, it was *my* hair??" William gagged.

His head dropped again.

"Bill, you probably won't have to buy a hair blower every other week," another comforted him.

Having just heard the news, a cheerleader came running to William shouting: "William! Oh William! Why did you?? How could you??"

"Sally, I needed the money," he confessed, fighting back emotion. "Look. My dad gave me 50 dollars to cut my hair."

The kids gave William pats of sympathy, shook their heads, and shuffled away.

"Hey, Man, you sold out for a lousy fifty bucks," one called back over his shoulder.

"Some give blood. I give hair," he yelled back.

A buddy came up with a ski cap. William pulled it over his ears, stumbled away, and murmured something about being bald at 14.

A Christian teacher
is one who just can't get
used to the idea of a
kid spending eternity
without knowing
Jesus Christ

The Cross at My Classroom Door

"What are you doing??" Darren demanded as I stood silently over his desk before the class bell.

I paused for a second to finish my unspoken prayer.

Darren, hostile and sulking, goes to junior high school in my blackboard jungle. Before the class period I prayed by his desk.

"Lord Jesus, this thirteen-year-old hates me because I am a teacher. Jesus, give me the exact love for Darren that You have for him.

One day I asked Darren to see me after class to discuss his semester grade.

"Darren, you only have to do one assignment to get a passing grace. Just one. I'll help you with it!" I smiled.

"You ugly witch!" he screamed at me.

His eyes penetrated mine with growing hate. He grabbed the scissors from my pencil holder and raised it in his fist. Holding it so tightly, his knuckles turned white and his face muscles, twisted at the mouth and eyes, gave him a demonic look.

"Darren," I said calmly, "if you would cut me into a pool of blood, I'd still care about you and love you."

"You dirty liar!" he shouted as he flung the scissors against the blackboard, ran out of the room, and muttered an obscenity at me.

After school that day I found a hand-drawn sign half the size of the door taped to the outside of my classroom.

Ugly monster-like creatures with horns and distorted faces had my name on them. A cross, drawn with lewd and obscene remarks about my religious beliefs, dominated the paper. A sick feeling flooded me.

I felt cut into raw pieces by rejection.

"Jesus," I said, "people are reaching to the Cross the same way today."

The next morning I taped this letter under the poster:

Dear Student,

The cross you blasphemed in the above sign was treated the same way nearly two thousand years ago. Jesus Christ was hanged on a cross like the one you drew. Those who hated Him laughed in howling mockery. He was hanged raw, bleeding, and naked. Yet He forgave them! Man, that's love!

Why did He do it?? He saw generations of messed-up lives — like mine — who needed a Savior.

Won't you stand at this Cross and ask Jesus Christ to come into your life?? He wants to call you His very own.

With love and forgiveness
because of Jesus,
Miss Witte

Darren dropped out of school two days later. I continued to bring him before the Throne.

Three years later I looked up from my desk and there was Darren. He had grown into a young man, and I knew something else happened to him.

"Miss Witte," he pressed before I had a chance to say hello. "Do you remember that poster I put on your door three years ago?"

"Yes," I nodded, still amazed by his new appearance.

"Well, I became a born-again person in an inner-city ministry. I came to ask your forgiveness."

Stunned, I got up from my chair, walked around the desk, and opened my arms, and knew Love had truly overpowered the hate in this boy.

Find Somebody to Love Lonnie, Lord

Lonnie and I talked about God often last year.

He asked Jesus into his life.

He was smart,

But painfully impatient with other kids.

He'd sigh and roll his eyes to the back of his head when they'd answer the questions too slowly.

And the sports heroes taunted *him*, because he couldn't finish the mile or hit a run.

This year I prayed,

"Lord Jesus, Lonnie's in high school now so You've got to find some other teacher to love him.

Somebody who will love him through his adolescence and insensitivity.

Somebody who will listen to him after school . . . in spite of papers to correct and grades to average.

One who will visualize his becoming the lead in the class play, student body president, and a great scientist.

Lord, You know he's going to learn to build up the egos of the less brainy kids.

And he'll admire the jocks for their talent, too.

But until then, Lord, You've just got to find somebody to love Lonnie!

When Christi's Dad Lost His Job

"Christi! Trust *our* God. He'll give your dad a job. God will give you everything you need, Honey. That's a promise," I whispered to 13-year-old Christi as her eyes filled with tears.

"Christi," I continued, "I trust my Father." I told her why.

"When I was growing up I would say: 'Dad, I'd love a new coat! I think I even need one!'

"There was no screaming, pleading or begging.

"When I was hungry, I didn't become hysterical thinking there would be no food on our table. It was always just, 'Please pass the roast.'

"When my young heart was being cut open with a problem, I'd talk to Dad. He may not even say a word. But he was always there to listen. And he didn't listen while reading the paper—even if I'd talk about trivia, he'd listen as if it were a life or death matter.

"Never once did I have to ask for money. Dad would automatically leave it on my dresser or press it in my hand.

"When I needed warmth and love, I just got close to Dad in his big reclining chair and said, 'I love you, Dad!'

"I didn't cry wildly 'to see' or 'feel' his love. It was always there. No doubt. Ever.

"Now when I cry out to God in desperate tantrums,

it may be because I needed the loudness to mask my fears.

"Momentarily, I forgot God is my Father."

Christi smiled and walked out of the classroom.

The next day she stopped by my desk and said shyly, "I trust my Father."

"I trust our Father, too, Honey." I whispered back.

From Your Son's Teacher

Mrs. Deane: Today your 12-year-old boy entered his first day of junior high school.

After his physical education class, he came to my English course.

He was wearing a sweaty t-shirt.

His hair was wet and perspiration slid down his summer tan.

He lacked self-control.

His buddies were loud and rough, too.

Their pencils were unsharpened and they left their notebooks in gym class.

And I suspect, Mrs. Deane, that your boy would rather be on his skateboard than finding the direct object of a sentence. . . .

Or be making a tree fort with his buddies rather than reading Emily Dickinson.

But I know that your son *will become* a beautiful young man in my eyes,

Because I will be asking God to give me *His* love for *His* child.

I promise you I will find ways to make your boy feel important, successful, admired, and loved.

Because you see, Mrs. Deane, I have found that loving a boy and building up that fragile adolescent ego means more in a life than diagramming sentences or writing in iambic pentameter.

Student Law

There are unwritten laws among students for which violation means social suicide. One must learn by careful observation and follow the code of appearance to the letter of the law or face unrelenting harassment.

One poor victim never seemed to catch on. And the carbon copy kids in their jeans, T-shirts, and Adidas spotted Arnold. Immediately.

Arnold, a class brain, crucified himself the first day of school when he sprinted into a ninth-grade class swinging his Samsonite leather brief case.

His next violation: wrong pants. He chose tailored slacks—not jeans—with a color coordinated belt and shirt.

When the cold weather came Arnold wore a fur lined hat with a bill . . . that snapped over the ears. And five-buckle overshoes.

"Arnold, Baby!" one jean-clad slave to fashion began, "you don't . . . you *just don't* wear a hat and boots. Baby, get with it. Man, if these kids see you, you'll be creamed."

Arnold dusted the snow off his hat and tucked it in his locker, "That's too bad. I prefer to keep warm and dry."

"And Arnie," another standing at the locker pressed, "we wear our jeans *on our hips.* Baby, you've got your pants up so high you'll have to zip down to talk."

"Arnie, baby. Stay out of those clothing stores. Please?? Get to the Goodwill. We're trying to help you, Man," the first encouraged, patting Arnold on the shoulder.

Arnold pushed the boys out of his way. "I do not care to have the individuality of slices of Wonderbread. So there."

By the end of the year, Arnold had been joked about mercilessly.

One spring day Arnold surrendered bravely, thinking he would have social success. At last.

He was wearing tennis shoes and jeans.

"Arnold. Arnold. Arnold," I thought to myself. "It's over."

His shoes were *clean*.

His jeans were *new*.

His social success: Terminal.

Take A Risk—Say "I Love You"

"Kevin, you failed this quarter! Do you know why?? I'll tell you why, because you failed every assignment. Every speech. Every test. Every quiz." I said.

"Kevin," I paused as the Holy Spirit reminded me of this kid's hurt. Changing my sarcastic words, I continued. "This next quarter you will succeed. I believe in you. You have failed, because I have failed you. I do love you no matter if you hate me."

"I do hate you and the whole stinkin' school," he seethed and stomped away.

"Kevin!" I called grabbing his arm, "please forgive me for not being sensitive to you the first quarter."

"I didn't realize until I made out the quarter grade you were going to fail," I continued as my voice cracked with emotion. "Look. I love you and I want you to love yourself and be successful."

While he jerked his arm out of my hand he left yelling, "Whadda' you afraid of? Ya think I'm going to slit your tires?"

His buddy who was waiting for him in the hall asked, "What did Witte have to say?"

"Heck. She said she loves me. What a liar. My dad hates me. My mom hates me and the cops hate me. Every teacher hates me, too, because I am a failure. Witte just said she loves me, 'cuz she's scared I'm going to wreck her two-bit Pinto . . . and I just might," I overheard him say to his buddy.

Kevin was another kid who hated himself because he never had any successes at school, or praise, or even a kind word. He made it obvious he hated school by constantly being hateful and muttering cuss words.

The next day I gave the class 15 vocabulary words to study for a quiz. Kevin, of course, was sulking and mumbling his disgust for me.

I leaned down and whispered in his ear, "I'm going to give you only five words. I know you can get a perfect paper! And Bob will help you study!"

I held my breath. I had risked my dignity. Would he lunge out and yell obscenities and humiliate me in front of the class? I shuddered.

"Forget it. I'm not doin' it." He grunted pushing me away.

"Jesus! Help Kevin and help me!" I said loud enough for Kevin to hear. (The class was studying by drilling one another out loud.)

"Kevin! I know you can get an A! Your goal will be only *five* words!" I told him again. "And I will pray for you."

An actual ray of hope flowed through his face. At last he realized he could have a fighting chance at success. He was given a target he could reach.

Bob and Kevin took the list and bounced to the hall. A few minutes later, I returned to them and asked, "Are you ready to write that 'A' quiz?"

"Almost," Kevin said with a lift in his voice that said he was near the longed-for feeling of being a winner.

"Yeah, he's almost got them! Could you give us five more minutes?" said Bob, the kid the class called Einstein.

Kevin broke out into a wide smile as I said yes. Then he quickly caught himself and wiped off the smile. His anger riveted through his body once again.

"I ain't doin' this stupid thing," he groaned, throwing the list on the floor.

Kevin realized he was risking something. He wasn't ready to risk and open himself up to love and a stab at success only to fail again.

"He feels I won't love him if he doesn't succeed at this quiz. Then he will feel worse torment and rejection," I empathized, feeling his agony. "Kevin, please come here," I called him over privately while Bob, who always felt loved and accepted because of his winning personality and brains, waited.

Emotion began to well up in my throat, as I began, "Look, Kevin, I will love you even if you fail this quiz. You aren't a failure in my eyes. I see you as a wonderful boy that God created. Just because you can't memorize the vocabulary words of the theater does not make you a failure. I heard you were a real brain when it comes to fixing engines. And listen. Even if you couldn't fix engines, I still would love you."

I couldn't believe what I was seeing. This tough, hardened kid's eyes were swimming. For his pride and image, I secretly hoped one of those tears would not betray him and come rolling down his cheek.

Bowing his head, and holding his emotions, he shuffled his feet. I touched his shoulder and silently walked back to the room.

"If he does fail this quiz, he will never attempt anything again," I thought.

The world was devastating for a kid like Kevin. We live in a society of "high-achievers" and "super kids."

But Kevin could never begin to compete with those kids, because he was just an ordinary kid with an over-sized need to be loved.

"Dear God, help me to see every kid as valuable just because he's a human being. Help me not to have human worth hinge on anything. Help Kevin to see my love without specifications," I prayed during the quiz.

Kevin did get a perfect paper on "his" quiz so I wrote a big red "A" on the top of the paper with this note at the bottom: "Remember I believe in you and you still would be loved even if you did not get this big beautiful 'A'! Love ya', Miss Witte."

Kevin didn't always get "A's" on the future academic targets I set up for him, but he always passed and that brought new self-esteem and confidence to him.

I learned something. A kid can make it through life, I am sure, if he doesn't know the vocabulary of the theater, or how to do a pantomime—but he can't make it without self-confidence.

I believe we should squeeze every ounce out of a kid in regard to their learning potential. Now it might defy all educational theories, but because of Kevin I found that love and self-confidence is more important than what I'm trying to teach in the classroom.

It's a funny thing. We teachers spend countless hours creating new learning programs, individualized instructions, and self-paced learning. We spend years taking education classes to help us teach problem students.

But simple love, a plain, ordinary, "I love you" is sometimes the best way to reach a kid. (And sometimes, the only way.) Just ask Kevin.

Tracey

Tracey doesn't have to wear her three-cornered scarf to cover up her head anymore.

Her baby-fine hair is growing back in soft curls.

And her already round face is only slightly puffy these days.

In September the principal's office let me know

Tracey had leukemia.

Now she is in remission.

But how long does this thirteen-year-old have to live?

I ache inside for her.

She hands me her assignments early and interviews people for extra credit on her tape recorder.

She comes into class and asks how my day has been going in her shy way...

but doesn't let her brown eyes meet mine for too long.

> *"Dear Jesus, I will be with Tracey for three more months. Open a way for me to give Your Name to a dying child who wants to live."*

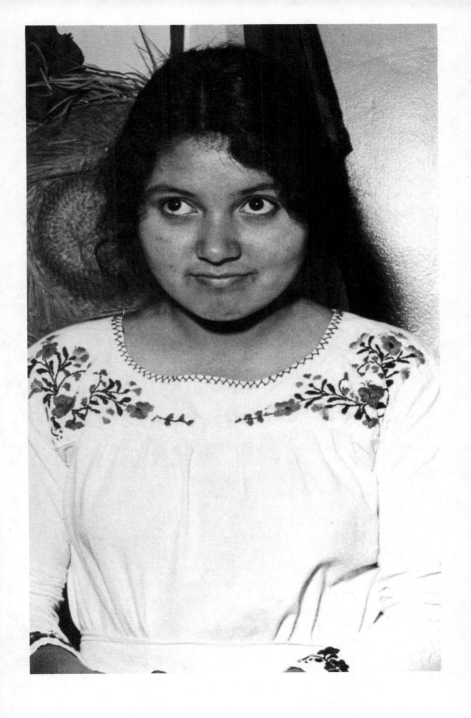

When Todd's Mom Came Home

"Something will stop you, Mrs. Grady. Your frantic campaign for glamour, riches, and romance will end," I said to her mentally as she left Todd, my student, at my apartment for a Saturday party.

Todd jumped through the door upon seeing the other kids drawing posters for the first party game.

Mrs. Grady walked down the hall of my building. I watched her jiggle out in tight jeans, high heels, and a tank top. She was braless and carried a short fur jacket over her arm. Long hair bounced down her back as three-tiered Indian earrings jingled. At the door she slung her fur coat over her shoulders and slipped into a small sports car.

"Jesus, stop her running. Her family is suffering and being destroyed!" I prayed until I saw her drive away.

But Linda Grady was not to pull out of my life. The eight kids filled my living room with laughter, games, singing, and contests on that March afternoon.

"Jesus, spare Todd from the sin that is preying on his mother. Close his young eyes. He's only twelve. . . . God! I fear for his future. Break those patterns and chains of sin so this handsome, rugged pet of mine doesn't have to be

destroyed by it!" I prayed inwardly as I caught glimpses of Todd throughout the afternoon.

I stuffed the eight kids into my Pinto and drove them home after the party. Todd was the last. The other kids ran into their homes with hands full of goodies, prizes, and posters.

When Todd opened the car door, he looked up at me with helpless eyes. "Bye," he muttered.

"Bye, Todd! You were so much fun to have at the party! The kids really love you! I was impressed when you shared one of your chocolate prizes. I was proud of you!" I said trying to relieve the sadness of saying good-bye as well as reinforcing him.

"Wa-a- that other kid, Mick, didn't win anything. That's why I gave him one of my prizes," he answered, secretly proud.

"I was proud of you. Now let me know how the football game goes! I am also proud of your playing!" I called out of the window before driving away. "Greet your parents. Thank your mom again for bringing you over!"

"And, Oh, God, . . . wake up Linda Grady. For this outstanding kid's sake—if nothing else. She doesn't even 'see' him," I whispered, watching him.

Todd walked slowly to his front door. With his head bowed, he smashed and then kicked a pop can as if to make a statement on life.

"Did he understand what his mother was doing? Were these his first signs of *his* becoming a cynical, hardened teenager that would emerge from a sensitive 12-year-old ripped apart by the raw, sin-sick world??" I wondered.

"Jesus! Stop Linda Grady! Hold Todd close to

You!" I demanded, pounding my hands on the steering wheel as I drove down the street.

In September of that year I had received a telephone call. My mind rehashed it.

"Hello, Miss Witte, this is Todd Grady's grandmother. Ah . . . you don't know me, but I had to talk to somebody," she began crying.

"I'm glad you called. Feel free to share," I answered, shaken by the prospect of what she may be reporting.

"Was Todd injured or killed?? Had I done something??" My thoughts raced while she cleared her throat and blew her nose.

"I ah-a-a I know you are a born-again Christian. I've heard you on the radio, and well, I ah-a-a just had to tell you about Todd' s mother, my daughter-in-law. She ah-a-a needs . . . prayer. She doesn't realize she's on the edge of s-s-sh-shattering lives—her husband and her three young sons," she stuttered and broke out crying again. "But I want you to know my three precious grandsons have prayed with me and they asked Jesus into their hearts. And I send them to Sunday school."

I listened. My insides began to clutch. I could only whisper the name, "Jesus," as she continued.

"Linda left my son. She lives with an older rich man who takes her to fancy restaurants and vacations all over the world. . . ." she hesitated, "I begged my son Dan not to marry Linda when they got engaged after high school. Dan was brought up in our Christian home. Linda was not a Christian. Oh, I've begged her many times to ask Christ into her life."

"Did she ever?"

"No. She always said, 'I don't want your Jesus. Stay out of my life.' "

"Listen. I don't mean it in a flip, cliché way, but I'll pray hard for her. Please trust me for that and I will continue to love Todd and believe in him," I pledged as we hung up.

Months after the party, I relived seeing Linda with her "stop-me-I-dare-you" attitude, as she left Todd and bounced down my hall.

Later that day, I received a phone call in school. "Miss Witte! I have to see you today! After school okay??" A frantic voice shook, "ah-a-a this is Todd's grandmother ca-a-lling."

"Mrs. Grady! What happened?? Something's wrong! Is it Todd??" I gasped, catching her panic and remembering Todd had been absent from school that day.

"I-I-I a-a-ah can't talk right now, Mis-s-s Witte. Just pray. Please pray for all of us," she sobbed.

Throughout the class hours I struggled guessing what dread thing might have happened. I alternated the gnashing with prayer.

Mrs. Grady was pushed as the students pressed through the door at the 3:00 P.M. bell. A hanky was wadded in her hand.

"Linda was vacationing in the south of France with this man. . . . " she began; "there was ah-a an accident."

Again I listened, watching the depth of human hurt and pain screaming inside another's body.

"She may not live . . . she's paralyzed. Her face is cut up."

"Mrs. Grady, dear . . . " I inhaled, "Dear God! I claim Your strength for all of us right now! God! Hold these people up!"

"She and her man friend were just walking down

the street and some drunk in an old truck slammed into a building and pinned Linda."

"What about her man friend??"

"He didn't get a scratch."

"Where are they now? Is he with her?"

"Linda was flown to the University hospital. I'm going back over. I just had to talk with you. And . . . that creep! That rat of a man. He left Linda to fly back by herself in an air ambulance. He's still vacationing. What does an animal like that want with a woman who is paralyzed?" she raged, "What are we going to do? Why did God allow this to happen?? Why?? I always prayed that my son and grandson would get their mom back. . . . "

"They will. And Jesus will get his child back, too," I determined. "How's Todd taking it??"

"He cried so hard when his father and I told him. But he wanted to shut his bedroom door and cry alone. You know boys. They're taught to be tough. After being alone for about an hour he came to me and asked, 'Do you think Mom will come back to us for good now?' "

It's impossible not to feel your insides falling out with hurt when you stand in front of a class and look into the face of a 12-year-old like Todd and know what he has to carry in his heart.

"Jesus, make him brave. Use this tragedy to seal his commitment to You," I prayed.

"Todd," I said one day stopping him after class, "you are brave. I am proud of you. Be strong and help your dad. He needs you. I will bring you a hot dish for your supper tonight. And Todd, remember, I believe in you. I think you're great. And never forget: Whatever our God does, He does in love . . . even when we don't understand Him."

I took him by the shoulders and said with my eyes the other words I didn't have.

"Todd, stay true to Jesus. No matter what," I finally whispered.

"I will. No matter what," he confirmed, looking down and swallowing back tears.

Linda spent the next year in the hospital. Todd was not in my class, but he stopped in often. He didn't talk much.

"Miss Witte! My mom's comin' home!" he announced, out of his usual quiet personality.

Breathing heavily, he ran through the classroom door. Although he was in front of me, he yelled: "I've gotta be there when she gets home! I gotta go!"

"Todd! Wait!" I said, grabbing his arm, "I'm even more proud of you! And I heard you made two touchdowns at the football game! Todd, WOW! You can be a Christian athlete when you grow up!"

"I'm already one!" he answered, puzzled by my thinking he was not a Christian athlete right now!

"Jesus! Heal as only You can heal," I said out loud, watching Todd run across the school yard.

Linda did come home.

But it hadn't been an easy journey. She hated God. She spent her months in the hospital bed cursing Him for taking her body.

But one day God's Spirit opened Linda's heart, and He used a 12-year-old boy.

"I asked my mom to pray with me and ask Jesus into her heart like my grandmother did with me. And she did," Todd told me without emotion shortly after his mother came home. "And my mom's going to stay home now, too, always and forever. She promised me and my brothers and my dad."

Of course, my first reaction was to cry.

"Wow! Praise God! Hallelujah!" I laughed, giving him a hug.

"See ya' later!" Todd yelled over his shoulder, running faster than ever out the door and across the school lawn.

Strive for Strokes—Or Souls?

"Lord Jesus! Get me out of this job! I can't take it! I try to please my principal! I'm too tender for the working world. And while I'm at it, why don't You give me a husband so I don't have to be out here getting kicked around?" I told the Lord as I walked out of Mr. Blake's office.

I had been called in to get chewed out.

"Come in, Miss Witte," he said, walking over to close the door behind me, "I want to speak to you about a tasteless comment made at your play this morning."

While he walked from the door to his desk, the scenes and lines of the play flashed through my mind like microfilm.

"Did some innuendo slip by me? (I had cut out even the slang words.) What did he hear?" I panicked.

"Your student directors said: 'If this audience doesn't show respect for the actors, *we* will stop the play and send you back to class.' Who do they think *they* are? What authority do they have? They should have said: '*Mr. Blake* will send you back to class and stop the play,'" he said, leaning forward and placing his fist firmly on the desk.

Then he got up and held the door open for me. His

body language said he refused to hear any explanation.

"I'll see that they change it," I whispered.

By the time I hit the word "change," I heard him shut the door behind me.

"Why didn't I defend myself? The kids chose the wording, NOT me. Why didn't I say that to him??" I beat myself.

Two weeks ago Mr. Blake told me I had been the most delightful teacher he had had in 30 years.

That compliment made me so high! I had been a better teacher!

Now I was crushed, on the bottom looking up.

"Lord! I know You're thinking I'm too touchy! Too sensitive! But I just got raked over the coals and creamed for something I didn't do! I can't control every kid's word choice! And the poor kids! They weren't deliberately trying to be defiant and challenge HIS authority. Just get me out of teaching! I can't take injustice. My principal didn't even want to hear my side," I moaned; "why doesn't he confront the teachers who leave early every day? Or the teachers who resent his position. I'M THE ONE who sticks up for him by saying he is our authority and deserves respect no matter what his decisions are. I'M THE ONE who admires his leadership and tells him!"

I felt good and sorry for myself.

After the last performance of the play that day, Brian, one of the actors with whom I had shared Christ, gave me a grocery bag.

"Open it when you get home," he said shyly.

The auditorium was empty and the actors had gone. As I sat on the coach of the stage set, I opened the grocery bag indifferently.

I was whipped. And it wasn't from directing two performances either.

The memory of Mr. Blake's words and face stabbed me throughout the day.

Inside the grocery bag was a gift-wrapped package. Even though it was from Brian, I was too defeated to be delighted.

Brian was one of those lovable, teachable kids who stops to walk me to my next class and carry my stacks of papers. He's the kid who hushes the others when I'm trying to talk. I've prayed for his commitment to Christ, and I know it will happen.

As I read his gift card which said, "Thank you for all you've done for me. I never can repay you . . . ," my wounded spirit lifted.

Then the Holy Spirit reminded me of my purpose in life: NOT to win strokes, but to win souls.

"Oh! Jesus! Keep me in the heat of the battle—for Brian—and others. Yes! I will suffer injustice or whatever it takes to be here, because I want to bring Brian into the Kingdom. Jesus, I love Brian. I've labored on my knees for his salvation all year. I won't stop!" I prayed.

(It's amazing how the labor pains are forgotten when a loved one is born into our family of God!)

Keys

"Here, Chad!" I yelled, throwing the keys across the stage, "go open the costume room for the girls!"

Chad caught the keys from my wild pitch. He ran off the stage and rehearsal went on.

"I shouldn't have given the keys to a student..." I thought, remembering the school policy. "Oh, I'm right here. It'll be O.K."

Rehearsal ended. And on Friday, that felt extra good.

"Oh, Chad! Give me the keys before you go!" I called as he was going out the door.

He dug in his pockets, shook his jacket—thinking they may have gone between the lining. His face flushed bright red.

"I don't know where they are, Miss Witte."

"Well, you better find them." I insisted. "Your buddies will have to go without you. You're staying here in this school until we find them."

Two hours passed. We had rummaged through smelly boxes of old costumes and fabric. I called to Mick, one of my custodian friends.

"Mick, I'll bet the keys got thrown out! Where do you dump your garbage and trash?"

"I've got about ten bins. Do you mean you want to go through it?? With your hands?" He cringed.

"Mick, I'm in trouble if I don't find those keys. I

gave them to Chad," I said, almost crying.

"Chad," I called, "come out of the costume room; you and I are going to go through the bins of trash! Especially you."

"Yuck! I don't want to put my hand in junk from the bathrooms!" Chad gagged.

"Dig in, Buddy. You're a guy in trouble. No complaints," I demanded.

Another hour passed. Chad had dug through five bins and I sifted through the others. No keys.

Being exhausted and near an emotional breakdown, I told Chad to go home.

"Käaren, you know we have to notify the principal and the police in a case like this," Mick reminded me.

"You're kidding! Oh, not the principal! Not the police! Please, Mick, let me look a little longer. It's only eight o'clock."

"I'm sorry, Käaren, I have to lock the building." Mick was sympathetic, but firm.

"Let me use the phone quickly before you go, Mick," I choked.

"Hello, Wayne, I lost my car keys. Dear Wayne, you're such a friend. Do you think you could come and get me? I don't have my car keys," I cried.

"I'm praying for you right now. I'll be there in a few minutes. Don't you worry. We'll pray in those keys," Wayne assured.

During that agonizing weekend, I demanded that God reveal the whereabouts of the keys.

"Jesus! There's no other way! The police have been called! You know that when keys are lost a multi-million dollar building is in jeopardy.

100

It's a very serious thing! Jesus! I shouldn't have given those keys to a kid. I knew it was against the policy ... forgive me! But You've just got to let us find those keys!!!"

On Monday morning Mr. Wallace came down to my room. The Dean had reported that I gave the keys to a student ...

There he stood. He seemed to be seven feet tall. I put my head down and looked up at him.

He had every right to chew me out, to fire me. I expected it. What a position I had put him in! What an inconvenience and problem for an already overburdened man!

"Ah ... I could say, Mis-s-s- Witte," he began confidentially as not to humiliate me in front of the kids filling up my class, "you know you're not to give kids your keys. But ... I won't ... "

With my head still down and my eyes floating while looking into his, I wasn't prepared for his next move.

He lifted his huge arm, put it around my shoulder, and moved me across the classroom to the door.

I felt euphoric with a sense of relief and hope.

"It will work out," he said at the door, tripping back into his professional role.

God was bailing me out. God was giving me another glimpse at understanding *HIS grace*. And He used my principal.

There's nothing quite like it. Grace.

I continued to plead to God for the lost keys. Later that day, another principal, who rarely left his office, just happened to turn a corner and find two boys fumbling with keys in a locked door. Being in the business for twenty years, he could spot suspects. And when the guys saw him, jumped, and dropped the keys, it was a dead give-away!

"What a miracle! I prayed these in! There was no other way! You do believe in miracles now, I'm sure!" I laughed to the Dean as he moved the keys hypnotically in my face moments after they were found.

"And I want to tell you, Principal Wallace showed me incredible grace when I lost the keys! Why, I don't remember such grace since my salvation! See? Mr. Wallace is second only to God in the grace department!!" I continued, taking advantage of the opportunity to witness.

The Dean simply smiled and eased away. I stood on the empty stage with my back toward the seats, clutched the keys to my heart, lifted my head heavenward, and started singing "The Doxology."

Mr. Wallace stuck his head in the door at the end of my song and called, "You are the luckiest person I know!"

He smiled, and waved. I laughed from my shoes up!

Angels in Faded Jeans

*"She's got one month to live. Less than a
month!! Jesus!! Do something!!!" I pleaded in
anguish.*

The school year had just begun when we got the
report that my mother had a month to live.

"Jesus! God!" I cried, having to face the second day
of classes with my insides falling out with hurt. "How
will I make it?? How can I teach?? God, You've got to
heal her."

A funny thing happened that year . . . God pro-
vided some angels. Some were seen. Some were un-
seen.

I hadn't been able to sleep the night before. Now
the first hour bell was about to ring. My eyes looked like
raw hamburger and I felt nauseated.

The students shuffled in quietly, still intimidated by
the new school year. (That usually changes by the end
of the first week.)

I spotted a youngster from my church, one of the
group, in her faded jeans and T-shirt. How I needed
somebody to cry and pray with! Yet I couldn't fall apart
in front of a new student. She was too delicate, petite,
and reserved.

"Dare I share this?? I've got to! My mother is dying!
It's one more person who could persuade God to heal.

She is a believer... no matter how young she is. But Jesus! I can't burden and frighten a 13-year-old with death," I debated.

God's mighty Spirit seemed to put a sacred hush over the class. Maybe they sensed what was happening to my insides. Maybe it was actually the presence of Jesus himself as He held me close during those days.

There was even a reverence as I told my class the plans for the year and the rules of the classroom. Oftentimes, however, I had to turn around in the middle of a sentence. Facing the blackboard and acting like I was "looking for something," I'd regain control.

"You can cry at lunch. You can cry in between classes. Just don't make a fool out of yourself in front of these kids," I told myself. "Jesus, hold me up. You're my only hope."

I seated the students alphabetically. Little Amy just happened to sit next to my desk. When she saw her seat location, she pulled her long shiny hair away from her face and smiled at me.

In my pain, I wanted to grab this child and say, "I know you know Jesus. Will you please pray for my mom as if it were your very own mother??? Please?? Please??"

I wanted to fall into the arms of *somebody* and have them tell me God would heal my mother. I wanted somebody just to sit with me while I soaked up wads of Kleenexes—six thick.

I groped mentally for somebody on the faculty with whom I could just be during lunch or between classes.

"Oh, God, bring just one person. Just one," I pleaded.

"Käaren, I heard your mother was sick," said Arlene, the physical education teacher.

"Thank You, God, for bringing somebody..." I telegraphed, heavenward.

"Thank you, Arlene, for your interest. It's serious. And if you believe in prayer, I would appreciate your praying..." I began.

"Oh, yeah, yeah... I a-a-h believe in prayer. A-a-h sure. Well, I've gotta run... pick up my son. He's got to go to the orthodontist. He's been having such a horrible time with those braces of his...." she raced, telling in detail, blow by blow, the progress of his bands.

She fled out the door, either uncomfortable with my asking for prayer or too caught up in her world to care about a young teacher whose mother was sick.

> The gnawing thoughts and prayers were relentless: "You've got to do something! God! Jesus! You've got to heal Mother! She's only in her late 50's! You can't! You just can't take her and leave Dad alone. You know how much I love that man. I can't watch him suffer and grieve. Jesus, are you answering??? Father, God, this is your child Käären speaking. You've loved, saved, and rescued me. You made miracles happen before. But this one is the most important. You know that."

I had always tried to look professional, positive, and pulled together before my faculty. I couldn't break down now.

Suddenly my mind flashed to Loren, a warm, tall, respected teacher who made a bold Christian witness. When I lost the school keys, I went to his room and asked him to pray for me. He had assured me he would. He knew I was in big trouble. I remembered as I left his room, I cried. I don't know if it was because of his manly tenderness or because of losing the keys. Probably a little bit of both.

Remembering Loren's caring, I knew I could calmly and without emotion ask him to pray for my mother.

"No, you won't cry in front of him. He'd only feel broken and helpless," I guaranteed myself.

The thought of Mom dying was slamming and pounding in my head once again. I was screaming inside; the pain was indescribable.

I gave the kids a short writing assignment. Opening the Bible, I devoured the scriptures and promises that told me Jesus went to prepare a place that eyes had never seen or could even imagine. What hope it gave me.

"Maybe some official will come in and see me reading the Bible . . . " I panicked, "but it's my only hope right now. They'd have to understand."

Suddenly I began to laugh. A joyous expectation riveted through me. Somebody was behind me. I thought it was one of the students. Somebody was going to put their hands over my eyes and say, "Guess who??"

The joy grew and burst. I laughed right out loud. I just *had to* turn around to see who was there!!

The sun beamed through the window and a soft vapor of white light blended.

"It's You, Lord! I feel Your presence!" I half-laughed and half-whispered.

I was warmed and loved, being held closely.

I looked up and thirty-five faces were staring at me. I wondered why. Then I realized they were noticing the radiant glow on my face as I smiled at the sunlight.

"Oh, my children. If you only knew what I had just

experienced here in this classroom. If you only knew," I thought, putting my head down to read again.

Before the class ended, I scribbled Amy a note: "My mom is dying. Please pray for her. I love you. I am so blessed to have you in my class. God planned it. I know. And I know you walk with Jesus, too. Love, Miss Witte"

Sitting next to my desk, I knew Amy was praying for me; I felt it. I warmed myself with her loving smiles. She was a thirteen-year-old angel in jeans and a T-shirt.

After that first week, I called a substitute frequently as I wanted to be with Mom to pray for her healing. And maybe saying the dreaded goodbye and watching her slip into eternity.

Four weeks and two days in the countdown for my mother passed. Family members kept saying: "Käaren! You've got to give up. You've got to stop this frantic campaign. God is obviously not going to heal her. Face it."

"No! I'll never give up! She's my mother. What's a home without the mother?? She's the sunshine and the heartbeat of the household. What's Thanksgiving and Christmas without your mother??? And when I get married I want her there. And when I have my own children, I'll need her. No!!!! I'll never give up!" I'd scream back.

Continually in my mind, whether I'd be by her bedside or in front of the class, was the thought: "She will be loved and cared for . . . FOREVER."

At the one month mark, I was still returning to the classroom. But this time I only lasted a half day. I dropped off the lesson plans and left.

Mom's legs continued to swell; she was breathing

hard with her mouth open. But she was still beautiful. Her coarse auburn hair looked even thicker and richer next to the white pillow. Her rings fell loosely around her fingers. And nobody regretted the decision not to have the destructive chemotherapy.

She breathed her last words with effort, "Praise the Lord." A few hours later, she was gone. With raw courage and whispering the name of Jesus, Dad slipped off the wedding rings.

I was given the number to call for a long-term substitute teacher. I thought her name was Mrs. Green, a woman I knew was a Christian.

"This is Käaren Witte. My mom died this morning. I have prepared myself and my students for this day. The lesson plans are on the desk. I know you're a born-again Christian . . . so I know you'll be praying for me." I choked out the words on the phone.

"Yes, I'm a believer. And I give you my deepest sympathy, Käaren," she comforted and quickly hung up.

When I returned to the classroom, I found a long letter with scriptures that ended with: "Just rest, Käaren, in the everlasting comforting arms of Jesus. Loren and I have prayed for you. We love you. Mrs. Walstead."

"What??!!" I gasped, "who's Mrs. Walstead?? She wasn't Mrs. Green??? Good grief!"

I realized I had talked with a stranger when my mother had died. But evidently this was the loving born-again lady whom God had planned to take over my classes, love my students, and bless me.

I knew the faculty would be watching me. I had chances to witness before, but this was the acid test.

"Jesus, I don't want to hurt Your reputation. Let these people see how a Christian lives and dies," I would pray.

I didn't ask God "why??" Just "what?" I knew why.

The faculty had given money, so I wrote a thank-you note and put it on the faculty bulletin. I held my breath as I hung it:

> *My dear Friends:*
>
> *Thank you for the gift. How very kind of you to remember us.*
>
> *I want you to know the sadness I feel is simply because I miss my mother. But she was a follower of Jesus Christ. And she claimed the verses: "For me to live is Christ, to die is gain." (KJ Version) (Philippians 1:21) and "Whosoever liveth and believeth in me shall never die" (John 11:26, KJ Version).*
>
> *I know one day I will be united with her because I walk with Jesus Christ, too.*
>
> *Please know that you are loved and appreciated. By me.*
>
> *Käaren*

As the next days passed, reactions were warm and positive.

Angels of all sizes—"mistaken identity" angels, strong men angels, 13-year-old angels in faded jeans. I saw again that God really does plant His angels—of all sizes—even in the corners of our world.

An Unlikely Opportunity

I hate rock. I hate loud music. And after a hectic day in school, I want to go home. So does every other teacher.

When my principal assigned several of us to chaperone a dance, I thought, "Why didn't he ask me to chaperone something civilized like a play or a band concert?"

(Do you realize what three hours of pulsating, blasting music does to 300 already hyper junior highers??)

My first station was the girls' washroom where I was to watch for smokers, pill poppers, and drug sales.

With a book, I sat on the cold tile floor and began the vigil.

Fifteen minutes passed.

"Two hours and forty-five minutes to go!" I stewed; "after five years of college and three years of teaching, I shouldn't have to sit in the lav watching for trashy girls."

Occasionally, irritated teachers would meander out of the strobe-lighted dance. Looking at their watches, they would complain in some way to the principal.

When the washroom door would open, I would catch their unguarded faces.

We all hated being there.

When two hours and twenty minutes passed, the Holy Spirit began to speak to me.

How I had prayed for my principal! God's Spirit reminded me.

"Jesus, let him see You in me. Make me sweet and cooperative. I want to win him to Jesus Christ!"

How I had prayed for the loose girls I would see in the halls as they shuffled in torn jeans and tight sweaters while smelling of smoke and alcohol.

Now they were coming into the washroom!

As they combed their hair and whispered their secrets, I would watch them in the mirror and pray:

"Jesus, reveal yourself to this hard child of Yours. You're her only hope."

By the time the dance ended and "Saturday Night Fever" had vibrated through the wall for the last time, I had had the opportunity to bring these souls before the very Throne of God! Not the straight girls with flowers in their shiny hair, so much, but the wilder girls, who would try to find love in the streets someday. Maybe even tonight.

It was 6:30 p.m. Friday.

After the building emptied, my principal met with the chaperones in the hall.

"Thanks for your help, everyone!" he said waving good-bye.

Some groaned. One said, "Yeah, sure." The rest said nothing.

"It was fun!!" I called back.

My principal stopped cold. He seemed to play back my words and think, "She spent three hours in a damp girls' washroom on a Friday night and never took a break. And she said it was fun."

I jumped in my car, threw back my head, and laughed: "We did it again, Jesus!"

A Kid Named Randy

"I can't play football," Randy confided, "I'm not strong.
I weigh 110.
My dad loves football.
And I want my dad to love me,
I want him to think I'm brave and rough enough to tackle big guys who weigh 200.
But I like to grow plants. I won a ribbon in the state flower show!
But I didn't want my picture in the paper.
Because dads love sons who star in tackle football.
Not flower shows.
Don't they?"

A Real Person

Thirteen-year-old Amy confessed, "I can't think of Jesus like you do, Miss Witte. You think of Him as a real person, don't you?"

"Of course, He's a real person, Amy. I'll show you!" I pressed. "Listen to these stories!"

I told her about the time I was a short-term missionary in Korea, and my support money was dwindling. For weeks I struggled. How could I possibly earn more money in a foreign country when I already had a full-time assignment?

One night at prayer meeting I requested the native church to pray for my finances. The next morning I found an envelope which had been pushed under the door with one hundred dollars in it and a note that said:

To Käaren
From Jesus

See? Jesus is a real person. He just uses the arms, hands, and feet of other people on earth today.

We must think in terms of Jesus being a real person.

It may sound crazy, but I now love to sneeze in public! Because sometime a person will say: "God bless you."

"OH! But He has!! And I'd like to tell you about it!" I'll answer to my unsuspecting well-wisher!

I also take that "Gospel Line" and "hot line to heaven" literally!

"Hello Jesus. This is Käaren. Oh. You already know. Well, I'm sick now and I've got to teach all those kids today. Ah . . . You already knew??? Oh. Of course. You would. Look, I know that You're going to help me so I'll just say thanks ahead of time. I'll talk to You later. Wow! Thanks, I needed that, Lord Jesus. I . . . love You, too! Bye!"

And when I take those scriptures at night I say,

"Lord Jesus! How thoughtful and loving of You to write these letters to me! And thanks for making thousands of promises to me! I know You always keep Your promises!"

When you walk and talk and laugh and cry with someone, you *know* they are REAL!

Troy

It happened again! This ragamuffin of a kid crumpled a sheet of paper and made a perfect shot in the wastebasket while I was talking. The bolder classmates cheered. The meeker smiled gleefully.

Troy's nervous energy was a constant source of irritation. He was perpetual motion . . . banging his pencil, scribbling frantically, blurting out sarcasms or making animal noises. He would come in the class late, usually slam the door and push steel-legged desks together. He was often on the verge of plotting his next form of attack if I did not yell at him.

Troy wore the same faded red plaid shirt constantly. He had shaggy long hair and always greasy smudged glasses on a face that had more than a 13-year-old's share of acne.

As a result of this daily nightmare, I dreaded coming to school. I would cry and pray every morning for the Lord to change this miserable kid's behavior and attitude. I just could not ever let him or the class see me lose ground in our daily power struggles. I would yell continually throughout the hour:

"Troy, sit down! We see your sick need for attention!"

"Troy, close your mouth or get out of here!"

"Troy, quit making a complete fool of yourself."

I would send him out of the room, humiliate him, show him I was the one in charge . . . AND NOT HIM. I could not weaken! I had to act tough or lose the war! Kill or be killed! If I showed any weakness, I would lose the respect of the entire class! There would be total chaos!

In these anxiety prayers upon awaking each morning, our faithful God began to speak to me about my wrong attitude. (Of course, I argued for a while!) Then I confessed this horrible, hateful attitude (finally). I saw how pride and anger had oozed in me over this punk kid.

Then I began to see him in a new light. I realized that he had no successful experiences and this made him a foul-mouth junior higher and would make him a dropout in high school.

How he must feel the humiliation of failure! No wonder he's an emotional time bomb. He has the same emotional needs to feel important, significant, handsome, loved, and popular as the class brain or the adorable cheerleader.

After praying for special courage to do the "impossible," I took Troy out in the hall and asked what I had done to make him so rude, miserable, rebellious, and angry.

He just replied: "Nothing."

"Then why do you act the way you do?" I insisted.

He just sat there and said nothing. He only scrubbed the eraser nervously in small strokes across the desk.

God's Spirit was working. I began speaking with a bit of emotion in my voice.

"I know I have been wrong. I have not been loving and patient with you. I am an adult and you are a kid. I am the one who should not have been hateful and angry. Will . . . you . . . ah, forgive me?"

When I hit the words "Will you forgive me?", his shoulder and arm gave a surprised involuntary muscle jerk. Then he just gave a slight, barely audible snicker. No words. I asked again. Still no words.

The following days I saw a change! Not only had he been touched by my ASKING HIS FORGIVENESS but he was responding to prayer.

It is now late in the year as I write this, but before every class I stand by Troy at his desk and silently commit our hour together and his life to Jesus.

"In Jesus' name I pray that Satan be bound in this young life. Jesus, reveal yourself to this troubled youngster crying out for love and attention. His only chance in life is to find You as Savior. Give me a love for him that will lead him to YOU."

I'm watching him quietly read right now. I'm thinking that one day people will see his changed heart! And not just toward me or in a classroom! Won't this faculty be surprised!

So who will get the credit for this kid who goes from hatred and hopeless to successful and saved?

Not this teacher. The glory goes to God's Spirit who is never defeated, gently convicting and always available.

I think that God doesn't change others to make it easier on us. He changes us to bring others to HIM.

So thank you, Troy . . . my raggedy tough guy. *You* taught *me*. God has given me a love for you. I think you're funny! Your twinkling brown eyes give you a special charm. I think you're lovable.

I think you must have forgiven me. Thanks for that, too.

Hold Onto Paula, Jesus

"Paula doesn't have a mother," her father explained at a parent-teacher conference.

"Oh, I'm so sorry. Knowing this, I can try to help her more," I began. "I know how she feels because my..."

"That's not all, Miss Witte," he interrupted and coughed trying to cover up his emotion, "Paula's mother killed herself. And it was on one of the days that Paula had a fight with her mother before school. When she returned from school she found her mother—dead from a gunshot wound. Paula, then eleven, found the suicide note which said, 'Paula made me do this....' Of course, Paula has never been able to forgive herself, and well... she's just so mixed up."

"No wonder she's rarely in school," I thought to myself.

"She keeps running away." He cleared his throat, looking down.

"But she's only fourteen. Where does she go?" I gasped.

"Perhaps you noticed Paula is a developed girl and more mature than the other kids?"

"Well, she does seem worldly wise beyond her years," I said tactfully, thinking that she looked like a hooker.

"She calls herself ah... a street person." He pursed his lips.

I reached out my hand to his. "I promise you I will reach Paula. I believe in prayer . . . and I will pray for her."

Paula was different all right. She often came to school looking like she should be at a disco, wearing black satin slacks and matching a tight top with high heels. Her appearance and attitude made her the object of off color jokes and comments.

"Paula's going to be a stripper!" One boy called to her in a crowd in the hall once.

"She's already a stripper!" Another one chimed in. "Take it all off, Paula, baby!"

Paula kept walking. Cat calls followed her down the hall. She didn't seem to mind. In fact, she seemed to savour the attention.

I watched her when she was in class. Her dark eyes were glassy when they weren't darting nervously at others.

"Miss Witte, I can't wait to get a car. Then I can go anywhere I want," she once said smugly to me after class. "I can really have fun then . . . if you know what I mean."

"Where do you want to go?" I asked.

"Oh, I go to parties with lots of older guys," she said sighing at what she seemed to think was my hopeless naiveté. "I suppose you don't know anything about men, and parties, and getting high. You seem so ah . . . well . . . I . . . don't think you're 'with it.'" She laughed nervously.

"Paula, I am high on life. Because I have a reason, a good reason, to live . . ." I began.

"But you're a teacher. How yucky. How do you stand these screamin' immature weirdos?" she interrupted.

"Sure, I'm a teacher and my job is to teach these kids. But I'm more concerned about their lives than their speeches and reports. The most important thing I can do is influence a few kids for Jesus Christ."

"You can't preach religion here in a public school. You can't try to convert them, you know," she reminded me gleefully.

"Oh, I'm not out to change *them*. I'm working on myself! When I get more patience, forgiveness and love . . . well more like Jesus Himself . . . then they will feel it." I smiled, "Right now while you've been talking, Paula, I have been asking Christ to give me love for you. And you know what? I believe in you. Because Jesus Christ does. And that's good enough reference for me."

"Hey, I know you don't like funky people like me because we're individuals. I know you hate kinky people . . . so don't give me that garbage," she mocked.

"Look, Paula, I've talked with your dad, and he's had enough hurt in his life, so I promised him I would help you. I would like you, firstly, to speak more politely."

"Ha! You help me! Baby, you're so out of it!" she howled.

"I'll just say one more thing to you, Paula. I do feel love for you whether you believe it or not. I only see you as a hurting, frightened human being who needs my friend Jesus to love her."

"Oh, gads, a Jesus Freak. Give me a break. Listen, I'll do the stupid assignments just to get out of this hole, but don't talk to me about this Jesus stuff anymore," she demanded picking up her books and slinking away.

Paula was out of school more than she was in as she was gone for weeks at a time after our conversa-

128

tion. Occasionally she handed me an assignment and announced to me and anyone else standing by my desk, her escapades with the men and parties.

Once Paula hadn't been in school for four weeks, which was longer than ever before. It was hard for me to pray for her as I would tell God how she had the art of making me feel like an old maid school teacher with functional shoes. And she knew it.

"Jesus, give me the grace to pray. I don't have it," was often my prayer request when Paula would come to mind.

"Paula tried to poke her eyes out. She went on a bad trip, ya' see. She's in a hospital, but ah . . . nobody's s'ppose ta know . . . so ah . . . keep it quiet. She wanted you to know." Tracey, one of Paula's drug scene friends, muttered one morning before school, as she chomped on her gum.

"She wanted me to know?" I questioned. "But I thought she hated me. . . ."

"Naw, I think . . . ah . . . she digs you now anyway. She was crying on this bad trip, ya see, but she was saying something about you caring about her," Tracey said shrugging her shoulders and drifting out of the room.

After school, I stood over Paula's bed looking at red scratches on her blanched white skin. Her eyes sunk deep in their sockets and straggly skeins of black hair were matted to her head.

"The guys I go with say they love me. . . . You know, my father never once said that he loved me. And he never even hugged me. But I wouldn't want him to," she cried almost incoherently.

"Paula, my friend Jesus will put His arms around you; He will love you. Many times I feel lonely and say,

129

'Jesus, I'm lonely. Please give me warmth and fellow-ship right now.' And the loneliness lifts. Every time."

"But it won't happen for me..." she sobbed.

"Yes, it will. I'll pray with you now. Jesus is waiting for you, honey."

"No!" she screamed as she turned and stuffed her face into her pillow, while pounding her fists. "Leave! Just go!"

Before I left, I put my hand on her heaving back and whispered the name of Jesus.

Walking down the hall, I spotted a washroom and ducked inside. I was glad it was empty, because I needed to put my head on my arm and let the wall brace me.

"Jesus," I said out loud, "reveal yourself to this tormented kid. Now! Do it now! She's going to kill herself. Jesus, I give Paula to You. I've got to. It's too heavy for me."

After being released, Paula went to a child psychiatrist. But she didn't return to school.

"Tracey! Is Paula coming back to school?" I charged as she was coming in the door reeking of liquor and smoke.

"Paula ran away," she clipped without looking at me.

"But where?" I quizzed holding her back with my hand on her arm.

"New York City," she snapped pulling her arm away and pushing through the crowded halls.

I visualized Times Square with the bizarre collection of lost humanity loitering on its streets.

"Would Paula live in some drug-infested commune? Would she feel the haunting need for love and become a prostitute? Would she be raped, beaten, or die?" I shivered, thinking of the possibilities for this child who already had thousands of miles of hurt and hardness on her face.

Three years have passed since Paula came in and out of my life. So often I have prayed and thought: "Why didn't I do more for her? Why didn't I try to find her? She is a human being for whom Jesus died, too. Was I just relieved she wasn't my daughter or sister? Did I subconsciously think, 'This serves this rude kid right'?" I shuddered.

"Jesus," I pray, "my rotten pride always cuts into some of Your work. But You work in spite of me. Jesus, right now—whatever pit Paula may be in, let Your Spirit reveal to her that Jesus will love her. No matter what she is. Jesus, she hasn't had the example of the parental grace and love. So how is she supposed to get a glimmer of understanding of Your love? Hold her, Jesus. Hold her and forgive her like You do for me."

Good manufacturers
always include
instructions so that
all the pieces fit
together

(so does God!)

Charm School

"I'm going to charm school," 13-year-old Lori flaunted at Ellie.

"Why?" Ellie demanded.

"My mother thinks I'm too much of a jock," Lori admitted.

(She was prone to bulkiness as her 5' 3" frame must have supported some 170 pounds.)

"Yeah, and my brother said I could win the Heissman Trophy," she added.

"Maybe 'cuz he thinks you'll get a lot of passes!" Ellie giggled.

"I don't think that's what he meant," Lori insisted, annoyed at Ellie's tasteless humor.

"Listen, maybe you could be the first female quarterback in NFL history!" Ellie cracked.

"Look, Ellie, I'm sticking out charm school. My mother said it's her last hope for my being a glorious specimen of womanhood."

"I want to be a glorious specimen, too," Jean-clad Ellie mocked, putting her hands on her hips and strutting down an imaginary runway. "Aw, come one, let's toss a basketball before the bell rings!"

"O.K. But wait just a second," Lori said, "I have to pull down my slip."

She lifted her skirt, fished around for the crawling undergarment and yanked it down.

"Wow! Is pulling down your slip in public permissible in charm school?" Ellie gasped.

"I guess. As long as you keep your knees together," Lori assured her.

Why Are There Deformed Little Boys in Your World, Jesus?

"Oh God! Jesus! How can You allow a kid like Ronald to come into this world? Jesus, I hurt for this crippled, deformed human. It's too painful to watch him fight for survival as he shakes and his muscles jerk involuntarily," I prayed when Ronald was first transferred into my class, *"and how is this kid with garbled speech supposed to give speeches and do plays?"*

Before Ronald left after that first hour, he rolled his wheelchair over to my desk.

My eyes fell on his small specially-built leather shoes—without real soles and heels.

He picked it up instantly.

"About these shoes..." he forced the words out apologetically, "I do want to have shoes like the other boys."

I was embarrassed. "Oh...those look like good quality leather!" My voice jerked nervously into a higher pitch.

"Yeah, but I still want shoes like the other kids," he said attempting to smooth his tousled hair.

I hoped he wouldn't catch another unguarded moment and "see" what I was thinking and feeling.

I welcomed him to the class but he said he was nervous about giving speeches in front of people. Assuring him, I said he could just give them to me privately.

He was relieved. Rolling his wheelchair around, he smiled while saliva ran down the side of his cheek and neck. His underdeveloped legs dangled.

School and growing up has a way of beating us all up even if we don't have outstanding physical deformities.

And just as I feared, Ronald was fair game.

The next day I came into the room and two boys were doing a comedy routine to the amusement of a circle of girls.

"Hey, what does a Ronald Laffle doll do?" one set up the other for a punch line.

"You wind it up and it moves like this and drools . . ." the other imitated.

The girls giggled. One said in weak conviction, "Tsk. Tsk. Not nice."

The bell rang. There was no time to discuss the scene. Ronald rolled in.

This was the day the class directors of plays were to have chosen their play and cast. I had forgotten, but the four directors were huddled over the seating chart.

"We're ready to name our play and cast," one director announced, as he began to call off the names.

"Would Ronald be chosen? Did I even get his name on the seating chart . . . after all he didn't have a desk. The directors were some of the cruel jokesters," I cringed.

The first director named his cast. Ronald was not among them. The chosen group applauded and sprang to a corner of the room with their play books.

Ronald showed no outward signs of being rejected.

The second and third directors didn't select Ronald either.

Now his involuntary jerking increased, and I recalled my own humiliation when I was always chosen last for the baseball teams. But I guess I didn't know what real humiliation was. I wasn't a spastic kid stuck in a wheelchair.

I could force a group to include Ronald, but because of his sensitivity, he would know. (And I could just hear some immature, insensitive kid sighing, "Oh, OK, we'll let him be in our play." I couldn't risk it.)

"Maybe I should head this disaster off and send Ronald to the library immediately to research some independent project," my thoughts raced.

Now the fourth director named his actors while the girls squealed and one boy yelled, "Aw right!"

Ronald realized he had not been chosen, and he began to speak.

"What was he going to say?" I panicked.

"Ah . . . quiet everybody. Stop talking a minute. Ronald wants to say something, I think," I called with my hands cupped around my mouth from the back of the room.

Several kids continued talking. Soon the room fell into an uneasy silence as Ronald continued.

". . . I know I'm different from the rest of you guys. I can't talk very well. And I know you might think that it would be a drag to have a guy in a wheelchair in your play. But I could help direct. And well, the friends I have say I am a good friend. And they're guys just like you, I mean, they don't have wheelchairs or crutches and stuff. So I know I could be a good friend to any of you, too," he struggled with his tongue getting in the way, "and look, if you think my shoes are funny, well . . . pretty soon I'm going to get shoes just like you boys wear."

Every head was bowed, except for Ronald's. He sat

taller than usual with confidence in himself after his warm words.

I didn't say anything. "I'll let one of these hot shots follow that," I thought.

After the 20 second silence, one student director slammed his fist on his desk and shouted, "I've got a great play idea! We want Ronald in our group!"

"Over here!" the formerly cruel jokester motioned to Ronald.

Ronald held his dignity. He smiled and bravely rolled to the group.

"Would they continue to make mincemeat out of Ronald," I shuddered. "Would his words soon be forgotten?"

I felt like I was throwing him to a den of lions. I knew how easily a fickle junior high kid could be triggered into cruel hate and anger towards another.

"Ronald was so vulnerable now. He had risked himself. He had offered friendship and he showed he needed acceptance. How well I knew of these kids' capacity for rejecting and destroying the self-esteem of another—sending them to thoughts of suicide when they committed the unpardonable sin: saying they needed friendship." I anguished.

"Jesus, You made Ronald. God, he probably has been hurt so much in his life. How much can a deformed fourteen-year-old take? Jesus, Lord, he's out of my hands; I put him in Your arms," I prayed.

Occasionally, one of the leaders would boldly announce, "We're going to have the best play! We're going to win the prize!"

"Oh yeah! We're going to win. Your play will stink

next to ours," another would shout back.

Enjoying this banter, Ronald would howl in a hideous high pitch and his muscles quivered. While rehearsing the play, Ronald had a smile on his face that said he had a secret.

"Just don't get overconfident these kids like you, Buddy. Don't blow your cool and get giggly or they'll kill you," I said mentally to Ronald.

On performance day, Ronald's group asked to go last. Finally, the director came out and proudly announced: "This play is an original mystery detective story starring Ronald Laffle as . . . IRONSIDES!"

Then he paused with his head down and began again, "And . . . ah, I want everybody to know that Ronald is my friend. My good friend."

The curtain went up; Ronald rolled out. The audience cheered.

Throughout the play Ronald said only a few lines, but his character had strength and professionalism.

The curtain went down as the audience gave a standing ovation.

Like most plays, after the performance I sat in the empty seats reflecting on the production.

My mind went back to the first day Ronald wheeled himself into my class. I recalled being horrified by this pathetic trembling human being as well as on the day of casting.

"Jesus," I said out loud in the empty theatre, "thank You for helping little deformed boys be so brave. They teach so much. Ronald will never earn a letter in sports, be an award winning debater, nor will he date the adorable cheerleaders. So just keep him encouraged and proud and strong. We need him. He helps me see YOU."

You Never Know

In the spring of one year a wealthy family invited all their children's teachers to their sumptuous home for a reception.

The guests didn't talk at first.

There had been a slow, icy start. Walking into a home with a sunken living room and a winding stair case evidently stunned this group of teachers.

Finally, people filled in the gaps of embarrassing silence over coffee and dessert.

The man of the house fit in the citadel of the rich. He was a proud man who breathed in the satisfaction of being the only family to ever invite the faculty and entertain them so royally.

When he sat down next to me, I began asking him where he came from, what he did, and his hobbies. He savored another chance to expose more of his world.

Glancing around the room, I saw the others tugging at their clothes and jerking uncomfortably. Several kept checking their watches. Non-verbally, they were screaming: "Let's get out of here. It's a bore. This guy just wants to brag and impress us."

"Jesus, make something out of this phoney situation. We know the motivation of these parents. They didn't invite us over to minister to us, edify us, encourage us and show their love and

appreciation. That's for sure. This is a bomb," I prayed.

These people had to make a statement to show the world how rich they were. And now they chose to impress teachers in Hush Puppies and polyester.

This was one of my lonely times. I would have loved to have had a Christian buddy with me. A comrade. A good friend. Somebody with whom I could pray and confide in. (I mean, I just couldn't reproduce this disaster talking to someone who hadn't been there!)

I had prayed so often for a Christian to eat lunch with, and to share some of the absurdities of teaching junior high, but God never chose to answer that prayer. Yet, now I am glad. I wouldn't have known Him the way I do otherwise. And I probably wouldn't have gone through the years in my blackboard jungle with my hand in His. I just know it.

A strange turn of events happened at the party. The conversations picked up. People were now COMPETING to be heard! Somebody would start to speak and I would begin listening to them. Another would rudely interrupt and I had the nerve-racking decision determining which way my head should turn and to whom. (I was a candidate for the "good listener's whiplash." A rare malady, believe me.)

Finally the father of the house directed a question at me. He wasn't ready for my answer. (I think the question was merely his standard. For he was sure the answer couldn't be possibly beyond five words or ten seconds . . . whichever comes first.)

Little did he know . . .

"Tell me, Miss Witte," he began, sucking his cigar,

"what or who's important in your life?"

I couldn't believe it. The lead-in question. The moment.

"Oh! I'm glad you asked!" I nearly shouted to be heard above the noise. "The most important thing in my life in Jesus Chriii . . ."

Just as I hit the word "Jesus" a funny thing happened. Every conversation ended. Silence. Several waited for me to finish my sentence.

I gulped. And did.

". . . st. It is only because of Him that I can begin to love the kids and get through life."

I thought the conversations had been strained before. You should have seen them groping, gulping, and squirming now.

How do you make a transition after that?

One teacher, edging to get out five minutes after he arrived, cleared his throat, looked at his watch, and announced he must go. Relieved at the break to get out, others followed.

I was the last to leave. The father said as we shook hands, "I've just never heard anyone say what they did about their religion."

"Ah . . . it's not a religion, Sir. It's a relationship. Thank you for your hospitality."

"Oh, you fool, Käaren. You idiot." I ground my teeth and screamed as I drove home. "They may not stone you in the parking lot. But these teachers who suspect you of being somewhat of a Pollyanna will really kill you NOW."

The following week passed. No comments. I was holding my breath.

At the office mailbox one day I thought I was going to feel the first stone.

"Miss Witte... about the statement you made about Christ." Mike, the 6' 6" physical education teacher began.

"Yes, Mike?"

"I want you to know, Käaren, that I'm a Christian now, too. A born-again Christian. It surprised a lot of people on the faculty, because they knew me as a hard, cussing man. I just appreciated your sticking up for God like you did at that party."

"Oh, wow. You're a believer," I whispered, dazed.

His enormous hand patted me on the shoulder. He smiled and walked away.

"Dear God! Don't let these stupid tears fall out of my face right here in the office!" I prayed.

I raced to the phone. I had to tell somebody.

"Sandi! Sorry to bother you at work! But I just had to tell you! I found another believer in my jungle! Remember that teacher who used to hit kids and swear at them? That's the one! Wait 'til I tell you the story! Talk to you later!" I gasped.

"Dear God... ah... sorry about my chicken-hearted witnessing. Thanks for the new friend."

I floated back to my classroom, sort of praying, sort of laughing.

It's a Victory! (It Just Takes Longer to Look Like One)

"John Mettski?" I called.

John did not answer.

"Where is John Mettski?" I asked the class while taking roll.

"Yeah! The creep finally got kicked out!" one smirked.

The class roared and several clapped their hands and yelled, "Aw right!"

"The assignment is on the board. . ." I said, leaving the room and going out to the hall.

There was John shuffling down the stairs. His greasy black hair brushed and swayed against the shoulders of his leather jacket—that read "Kiss" on the back.

At the beginning of the year, I had asked him: "Why don't you get along with the other kids and teachers? Why do you seem to hate everybody?"

"Teachers hate me 'cuz I'm dumb. So I hate them," he scolded me.

(He was in eighth grade, but he was reading at a third grade level.)

"John, I don't think you're dumb. I want to make you the classroom assistant. You will be in charge of the tape recorders and running the movie projector.

You will also be in charge of the floors, so make sure the kids keep the debris picked up." I smiled and patted him on the shoulder.

"Big deal," he snorted, jerking his shoulder from under my hand and running away.

"Jesus," I had prayed, "John doesn't make it easy. He's so obnoxious and cynical. You're the only one who can help me find ways to make him feel important and admired."

The following months John did come into class to do his duties. He would walk up and down the rows instructing the others to pick up the scraps of paper, candy wrappers, and sunflower seed shells.

He seemed to feel needed and important finally, but he continued his rudeness. He'd never look me in the eye or answer beyond a grunt.

"John! John!" I was now calling catching a glimpse of him, "What happened?" I moved to the edge of the stair case and John looked at me for the first time.

"I got kicked out, but you've got to believe me . . . it wasn't my fault this time," he pleaded.

"Look, John, I believe you. And I'm going to tell the Dean that you've been a pretty good guy in my class so far this year. Maybe that will help."

His hard face softened, tears filled his eyes. "Thanks for thinking about me," he whispered reaching out to my heart for help.

At that instant, God's Spirit said, "Tell him you love him."

"What! I can't tell a kid like this I love him! Can you imagine what he would say to his other buddies: 'Hey, Hey! Witte said she loved me!' I'll be a push over . . . whipped creamed . . . a marshmallow! I'll lose all my authority in the blackboard jungle," I argued.

Again God's Spirit nudged me: "Tell him you love him."

"Ah . . . John . . . ah . . . look, thanks. Ah . . . I will be thinking more about you. I've got to get back to the room; I left the kids alone."

"Don't go," John said freezing his eyes to mine.

I reached down and held my hand on his head. I was trying to get the words out . . . "John . . . ah . . . I . . ."

His chin started to quiver and the tears fell out of his eyes. After he tried to wipe his eyes on his leather jacket sleeve, he used his wet, slippery fists again.

"John, I've got to go," I insisted.

"Jesus, why didn't I risk? Why didn't I take the chance and see what the powerful words: 'I believe in you and I love you' could do for a kid like this. Why didn't I say it?" I anguished, walking back to the room.

Later that day, I was correcting test papers from the week before and, of course, John had only scribbled his name on the top. Not one answer was filled in.

So I wrote across the paper: "Remember I believe in you and love you, John. Sorry I didn't say it when you needed it the very most. God is helping me with those areas. Just be patient with me. Love, Miss Witte."

John was allowed to come back to school on my recommendation the following day. When he came into class, I was handing out the test papers.

John read my comment and murmured foul words as he smashed and crumpled it loudly. After he had thrown it in the waste basket, he jumped in the basket and stomped the papers down farther.

John never did look at me in the eye nor speak to

me again. He refused to do the assisting duties while just pretending to do any class assignments.

I felt like a fool.

> *"Jesus, until You melt John's heart and spirit, I need Your love. Cover my loss of pride," I prayed feeling the burn of humiliation. "Give me the grace and forgiveness to bring him before the Throne. It's his only chance in life."*

Some rewards and victories take a while. We call them long range.

I've got to believe John's one of those types of victories.

Give someone a
shot of praise...
produces no harmful
side effects

Praise By Mistake

"He's an enthusiastic, colorful, articulate speaker for only thirteen years old," I thought as I listened to Bill's first speech performance on the second day of school in my junior high speech and drama class.

Bill told graphic stories that electrified the class—like his memory of jumping into deep water and learning to swim . . . quickly . . . at six years old!

The class listened and laughed. Bill felt proud, even loved. I could tell.

On the evaluation sheet I wrote: "Bill, you appear to be a bright, gifted young man. I am glad to see your talent in communicating! You know how to capture the imagination of your audience! You are also an intriguing storyteller! I am looking forward to all of your performances and speeches this year! You are off to a good start. It is encouraging to see a student motivated and using his intelligence."

The following week I was called to a meeting with the staff and Bill's parents to discuss students with learning disabilities.

I walked into the conference room and I was introduced to Bill's mother.

When she heard my name, her face glowed! "Oh! You're Billy's favorite teacher! Did you know that you were the first teacher that ever called him 'bright' and 'intelligent'? Why, he put your comment-evaluation sheet up on his bedroom wall. And his little brothers better not touch it!"

Her appreciation spilled out in more emotionally charged words. I was startled. Stunned. We teachers just do not hear things like this.

As Bill's mother was telling how thrilled Bill was to be recognized and praised, I noticed the principals, the psychologists, and other teachers raise questioning eyebrows.

They realized I had mistakenly called Bill "bright and intelligent"! After all, we were in this meeting because Bill had proven through eight years of school *NOT* to be bright and intelligent! He was writing and reading at a fourth grade level!

"What do these professional people think of me?" I gasped to myself.

"Oh, Lord, bail me out!" I prayed. "I've made myself look like a jerk. A real Pollyanna! How could I call this kid 'bright and gifted'? He has a severe learning disability and is a slow learner! Oh, if only I had studied his records and test scores and had seen his reading and writing skills, I never would have made such an unprofessional, stupid mistake. This will cost me the respect of my administrators and professional colleagues! They probably wonder what kind of a college and education department I graduated from when I can't even spot a slower learner with learning disabilities."

I left the meeting feeling humiliated. But in the following weeks, Bill not only did his oral projects, but he did them ahead of time! I assigned him to help other students. (They were not slow learners! They were just not motivated like Bill!)

Occasionally I would eavesdrop on Bill as he coached "his students" in the hall.

"Remember to use words that will put a picture in the kids' heads. Make the story exciting! They'll love it. Be sure to repeat your main points. You know, tell them what you've told them!" he'd remind them.

It is the middle of the year as I write this. Bill even reads and writes with new interest now...especially when it is going to be turned into an oral project. He is also going to have a role in this year's spring play. Bill is the most "turned on kid" in my speech and drama class.

"Lord Jesus," I now pray, "help me to see Bill as You do. He's Your very own. You made and BOUGHT him, too. Give me the power to encourage and admire all the 'Bills' in my life. Like You do."

The Holy Spirit often brings to mind: "Yet not I, but Christ liveth in me...." (Gal. 2:20). And with that truth, I will do it!

Praise changes people...even if it is by mistake.

Letter to a Former Student:

Dear Larry,

I think of you and your classmates often. The years have flown by since you were a junior high student in my class.

Larry, although you're in high school, I still pray for you. I'm excited about your future! You can be anything you want!

One day I will say to the world: "That's one of MY former students, Larry!" Maybe you'll be given an award, or become an outstanding businessman, lawyer, doctor, or minister. Whatever you choose in life, you will be successful. I know. And I'll be cheering for you.

I have confidence, because I have prayed for you since I first saw you in junior high.

I remember when you had the lead in the class play. I can still see you acting with wild emotion and singing! Did you know that you supported and encouraged me during those days of producing the junior high play? Your frequent, "Thanks, Miss Witte!" and pats on the back pushed me on and brightened the moments. Your cheerfulness made the late rehearsals and the frustration of some kids not knowing their lines fade somehow. The other kids saw that even a student could give encouragement to a teacher. (And teachers need encouragement, too!) They joined in—thanks to you.

Did you notice the tears welling up in my eyes the time you told me you went to your friend's summer camp and raised your hand to give your life to Jesus Christ? Jesus Christ loves you so much! He believes in you, Larry!

Other people may cut you down and you may cut yourself down. But every single second of every day Jesus Christ is calling out: "I believe in you, Larry!"

Jesus Christ intended you for greatness! So get ready! Do you think you have dreams and plans? I know you do. Terrific! But aren't you glad God doesn't rely on our puny imaginations? He's dreaming far beyond and above what we could ever dream or hope for! (Ephesians 3:20 says so! It's a promise. And Jesus Christ always keeps His promises!) Put big dreams on your list of things to do!

I will be praying for your family, and your relationship with them. Through their love, I hope you will just begin to understand the love of God! I will also pray for the friends you will make ... that they also will walk with Jesus Christ!

Dream big, Larry! Remember, small plans just don't have the capacity to change the world! Whatever you dream and plan for you will achieve. You can! You have Jesus Christ in your life! Never forget that!

And never forget that I'm out here believing you could be president of the United States, or anything you want ... if you put it ON YOUR LIST!

Keep in touch.

With love, prayer, and great memories,
Miss Witte

To My Friends:

Thank you for allowing me to share my experiences with you. I would love to hear from you!

If you have never asked Jesus Christ to be your closest friend and Savior, you may do so right now! He loves you. He waits for you. He has promised to come into your life. Just simply say, "Jesus Christ, I believe You are God's very own Son and You died for my sins. Forgive me for my sins. Make me a new person, like You promised I would be. I want to be born again."

The promise that you are born again is a FACT, not a feeling. Never doubt from this moment forward that Jesus Christ is in your life—even if you are sick, hurting, or lonely.

God's Spirit will tell you in your heart that you belong to Him (Romans 8:16).

Salvation happens at conception—the moment you receive the living God. You then belong to this great family of God. (Remember it's like your biological family. No matter what you do, where you go, or how you behave—you're still in the family! (John 3:16, 17)

If you have asked Jesus Christ into your life, I would love to hear from you, too. I want to meet the "new person" the scriptures promised you'd be! (II Cor. 5:17)

You may write to me in care of the publisher at 5624 Lincoln Drive, Edina, Minnesota 55436.

God bless you above and beyond what you could ever dream or hope for! (Eph. 3:20) Know that you are loved . . . by God and by me.

Sincere Christian love,

Käaren

Käaren Witte

P.S. I'll see you when we all get Home!